Better Homes and Gardens®
homemade
Gifts in a Jar

Meredith® Books
Des Moines, Iowa

Book Title

Editor: Tricia Laning
Contributing Editors: Spectrum Communication
    Services, Inc.
Associate Design Director: Chad Jewell
Copy Chief: Terri Fredrickson
Publishing Operations Manager: Karen Schirm
Book Production Managers: Pam Kvitne, Marjorie
    J. Schenkelberg, Rick von Holdt, Mark Weaver
Contributing Proofreaders: Arianna McKinney, Nancy
    Widman, Susie Kling, M.Peg Smith
Photographer: Blaine Moats
Food Stylist: Dianna Nolin
Indexer: Jennifer Champion
Editorial Assistant: Cheryl Eckert
Edit and Design Production Coordinator:
    Mary Lee Gavin
Test Kitchen Director: Lynn Blanchard
Test Kitchen Home Economists: Marilyn Cornelius;
    Juliana Hale, Laura Harms, R.D.;
    Jennifer Kalinowski, R.D.; Maryellyn Krantz; Jill
    Moberly; Dianna Nolin; Colleen Weeden;
    Lori Wilson; Charles Worthington

Meredith₀ Books

Editor in Chief: Linda Raglan Cunningham
Design Director: Matt Strelecki
Managing Editor: Gregory H. Kayko
Executive Editor: Jennifer Dorland Darling

Publisher: James D. Blume
Executive Director, Marketing: Jeffrey Myers
Executive Director, New Business Development:
    Todd M. Davis
Executive Director, Sales: Ken Zagor
Director, Operations: George A. Susral
Director, Production: Douglas M. Johnston
Business Director: Jim Leonard

Vice President and General Manager:
Douglas J. Guendel

Better Homes and Gardens₀ Magazine
Editor in Chief: Karol DeWulf Nickell
Deputy Editor, Food and Entertaining: Nancy Hopkins

Meredith Publishing Group
President, Publishing Group: Stephen M. Lacy
Vice President-Publishing Director: Bob Mate

Meredith Corporation
Chairman and Chief Executive Officer: William T. Kerr

In Memoriam: E.T. Meredith III (1933-2003)

All of us at Meredith₀ Books are dedicated to providing
you with the information and ideas you need to create
delicious foods. We welcome your comments and
suggestions. Write to us at: Meredith Books, Cookbook
Editorial Department, 1716 Locust St., Des Moines, IA
50309-3023.

If you would like to purchase any of our cooking, crafts,
gardening, home improvement, or home decorating and
design books, check wherever quality books are sold. Or
visit us at: bhgbooks.com

Pictured on front cover: Pretty Posy Jar (see page 58),
Gazpacho Salsa (see page 46), Cranberry-Chocolate Chip
Cookie Mix (see page 12)

Our seal assures you that every recipe in
Homemade Gifts in a Jar has been tested in
the Better Homes and Gardens₀ Test
Kitchen. This means that each recipe is
practical and reliable, and meets our high
standards of taste appeal. We guarantee your
satisfaction with this book for as long as you
own it.

Table of Contents

· ·

Chapter 1
Jar Gifts from the Kitchen

Ready-to-serve goodies and tempting layered mixes are winning combinations in this chapter devoted to foods and drinks packaged in canning jars. And the foods are so delicious. Cranberry-Chocolate Chip Cookie Mix, Lemon Tea Bread MIx, Caramel-Rum Sauce, and Spicy Barbecue Rub are a few of the recipes you'll want to share with family and friends.

Chapter 2
Jar Gifts from the Crafts Table

You'll look at jars with a fresh eye when you see all the fun things to make with them! Elegant fabric-wrapped vases, textured canisters, seasonal candles, playful banks, and more will spark your creativity. Plus find ideas for making paper gift tags and tips for inspiring kids to craft with jars.

May no gift be too small to give, nor too simple to receive, which is wrapped in thoughtfulness, and tied with love.

—L.O. Baird

The Joy of Jars

I admit it. I have an affinity for canning jars. I love the thought of transforming something simple into something wonderful.

Jars are one of those items that have endless possibilities. To start, they come in a multitude of sizes—perfect for containing prepared foods and ready-to-mix recipes as well as being blank canvases for paint, clay, and other crafting mediums.

I also like the fact that I can purchase canning jars just about anywhere. You can pick them up at grocery and discount stores, craft shops—even hardware stores!

These readily available, inexpensive, air-tight containers are thoughtful gifts when personalized with colorful tags, festive ribbons and thoughtfully written recipe cards. Presenting someone special with a gift you've created says "you mean the world to me."

This book shares dozens of fun ways to use canning jars. You'll run straight for the kitchen when you discover the delicious layered mixes and prepared foods that fit in a jar, such as Dried Cherry Scone Mix and Gazpacho Salsa. With so many new recipes to share, you'll want to have an extra case of jars on hand.

For your creative side, there's an artsy array of canning jar crafts: jars wrapped with fabric, clay, and jute; beautiful jar candles, vases, and organizers—even adorable clay-covered jar bird banks kids can make.

So if you thought canning jars were just for pickles—you'll be amazed with the spectacular gift ideas that let friends and family know how special they are to you.

Happy giftmaking!

Tricia Laning

1
Chapter

··

Jar Gifts from the Kitchen

Enjoy a delicious collection of recipes for
foods and mixes that use canning jars as the
"wrap." Your family and friends will crown
you queen of the kitchen when they are
presented with these wonderful homemade
treats—from soup and dessert mixes to
heavenly sauces and salsas.

Cranberry Drop Cookie Mix

The tart-sweet flavor and chewy texture of dried cranberries make these orange-accented cookies especially pleasing.

1⅓ cups all-purpose flour
1 teaspoon baking powder
½ teaspoon ground nutmeg
¼ teaspoon salt
½ cup shortening
⅓ cup packed brown sugar
⅓ cup granulated sugar
1 cup snipped dried cranberries
¾ cup chopped walnuts

1. In a medium bowl stir together flour, baking powder, nutmeg, and salt. Using a pastry blender, cut in shortening until mixture resembles coarse crumbs.

2. In a 1-quart glass jar layer in the following order: brown sugar, granulated sugar, cranberries, flour mixture, and walnuts. Tap jar gently on the counter to settle each layer before adding the next one. Seal; attach directions for making Cranberry Drop Cookies. Store in a cool, dry place for up to 1 month. Makes 1 jar (enough mix to make about 30 cookies).

PREPARATION DIRECTIONS To make Cranberry Drop Cookies: Empty the contents of the jar into a large bowl; stir until mixed. In a small bowl combine 1 slightly beaten egg and 2 tablespoons orange juice; add to flour mixture in bowl. Stir until combined. Drop dough by rounded teaspoons 2 inches apart onto ungreased cookie sheets. Bake in a 375°F oven about 10 minutes or just until lightly browned. Transfer to wire racks; cool. Makes about 30 cookies.

Oatmeal-Chipper Mix

TO MAKE THE MIX...

$^3/_4$ cup all-purpose flour
$^1/_2$ teaspoon baking soda
$^1/_3$ cup granulated sugar
$^1/_3$ cup packed brown sugar
1 cup semisweet chocolate
   pieces
1 cup rolled oats
$^1/_2$ cup peanut butter pieces

Oatmeal-chocolate chip cookies, a long-standing favorite, get a flavorful update with the addition of peanut butter pieces.

1. In a small bowl stir together flour and baking soda. In a 1-quart glass jar layer in the following order: granulated sugar, brown sugar, chocolate pieces, oats, flour mixture, and peanut butter pieces. Tap jar gently on the counter to settle each layer before adding the next one. Seal; attach directions for making Oatmeal Chippers. Store in a cool, dry place for up to 1 month. Makes 1 jar (enough mix to make 24 to 30 cookies).

PREPARATION DIRECTIONS

To make Oatmeal-Chippers: Grease cookie sheets; set aside. Empty the contents of the jar into a large bowl; stir until mixed. Add $^1/_2$ cup softened butter, 1 slightly beaten egg, and 1 teaspoon vanilla; stir until combined. Drop dough by heaping teaspoons 2 inches apart onto prepared cookie sheets. Bake in a 375°F oven for 8 to 10 minutes or until edges are lightly browned. Transfer to wire racks; cool. Makes 24 to 30 cookies.

Fudge Brownie Mix

1 cup all-purpose flour
1/2 teaspoon baking powder
1/4 teaspoon salt
1/3 cup unsweetened
    cocoa powder
1 1/2 cups sugar
1/2 cup semisweet
    chocolate pieces
1/2 cup chopped walnuts
1/2 cup white baking pieces

This mix is the first step to a batch of rich fudge brownies. No chocolate lover will be able to resist them.

1. In a small bowl stir together flour, baking powder, and salt. In a 1-quart glass jar layer in the following order: cocoa powder, sugar, chocolate pieces, flour mixture, walnuts, and white baking pieces. Tap jar gently on the counter to settle each layer before adding the next one. Seal; attach directions for making Fudge Brownies. Store in a cool, dry place for up to 1 month. Makes 1 jar (enough mix to make 16 brownies).

PREPARATION DIRECTIONS To make Fudge Brownies: Grease and flour an 8×8×2-inch baking pan; set aside. In a large bowl combine 1/2 cup butter, melted and cooled, and 2 slightly beaten eggs. Stir in the contents of the jar. Spread into prepared pan. Bake in a 350°F oven about 35 minutes or until edges begin to pull away from pan. Cool in pan on a wire rack. Cut into bars. Makes 16 brownies.

Blond Brownie Mix

1/2 cup white baking pieces
3/4 cup packed brown sugar
2 cups packaged biscuit mix
1/2 cup chopped
   almonds, toasted

Chock–full of almonds and white baking pieces, these golden bars are scrumptious with a cup of hot chocolate or tea. The packaged biscuit mix in the base makes it extra easy to assemble.

1. In a 1-quart glass jar layer in the following order: white baking pieces, half of the brown sugar, half of the biscuit mix, the remaining brown sugar, the remaining biscuit mix, and the almonds. Tap jar gently on the counter to settle each layer before adding the next one. Seal; attach directions for making Blond Brownies. Store in a cool, dry place for up to 1 month. Makes 1 jar (enough mix to make 16 brownies).

PREPARATION DIRECTIONS

To make Blond Brownies: Grease an 8×8×2-inch baking pan. Empty the contents of the jar into a large bowl; stir until mixed. Add 1/2 cup butter, melted and cooled; 1 beaten egg; and 1 teaspoon vanilla. Stir until combined. Spread into prepared pan. Bake in a 350°F oven about 25 minutes or until edges are golden and center is almost set. Cool in pan on a wire rack. Cut into bars. Makes 16 brownies.

Cranberry-Chocolate Chip Cookie Mix

3/4 cup all-purpose flour
1/2 teaspoon baking powder
1/4 teaspoon salt
2/3 cup sugar
1 cup semisweet
  chocolate pieces
1/2 cup dried cranberries
1/2 cup chopped pecans
1 cup quick-cooking rolled oats

If you prefer, make these colorful drop cookies with walnuts or macadamia nuts instead of pecans.

1. In a small bowl stir together flour, baking powder, and salt. In a 1-quart glass jar layer in the following order: sugar, chocolate pieces, flour mixture, cranberries, pecans, and oats. Tap jar gently on the counter to settle each layer before adding the next one. Seal; attach directions for making Cranberry-Chocolate Chip Cookies. Store in a cool, dry place for up to 1 month. Makes 1 jar (enough mix to make about 24 cookies).

PREPARATION DIRECTIONS

To make Cranberry-Chocolate Chip Cookies: Empty the contents of the jar into a large bowl; stir until mixed. Add 1/2 cup softened butter, 1 slightly beaten egg, 1 tablespoon milk, and 1 teaspoon vanilla; stir until combined. Drop dough by teaspoons about 2 inches apart onto ungreased cookie sheets. Bake in a 350°F oven for 10 to 12 minutes or until lightly browned. Transfer to wire racks; cool. Makes about 24 cookies.

Holiday Oat Cookie Mix

TO MAKE THE MIX...

2   cups all-purpose flour
1   teaspoon baking soda
2   cups white baking pieces
2   cups rolled oats
2   cups red and green candy-
     coated milk chocolate pieces
$2/3$ cup packed brown sugar
$2/3$ cup granulated sugar

The red and green candy-coated milk chocolate pieces make this mix just the thing for a stocking gift; it's also a terrific springtime gift when made with pastel-colored candies.

1. In a small bowl stir together flour and baking soda. In each of two 1-quart glass jars layer in the following order: half of the white baking pieces, half of the oats, half of the candy-coated milk chocolate pieces, half of the brown sugar, half of the granulated sugar, and half of the flour mixture. Tap jar gently on the counter to settle each layer before adding the next one. Seal; attach directions for making Holiday Oat Cookies to each jar. Store in a cool, dry place for up to 1 month. Makes 2 jars (enough mix in each jar to make about 36 cookies).

PREPARATION DIRECTIONS   To make Holiday Oat Cookies: Empty the contents of 1 jar into a large bowl; stir until mixed. Add $1/2$ cup butter, melted and cooled; 1 slightly beaten egg; and 1 teaspoon vanilla. Stir until combined. Drop dough by heaping teaspoons 2 inches apart onto ungreased cookie sheets. Bake in a 375°F oven for 8 to 10 minutes or until edges are lightly browned. Transfer to wire racks; cool. Makes about 36 cookies.

Ranger Cookie Mix

Kids can help measure and layer the ingredients for this longtime favorite, which makes a terrific gift for a special teacher.

1¼ cups all-purpose flour
½ teaspoon baking powder
¼ teaspoon baking soda
½ cup shortening
2 cups fruit-flavored
    crisp rice cereal
⅔ cup packed brown sugar
⅓ cup coconut

1. In a medium bowl stir together flour, baking powder, and baking soda. Using a pastry blender, cut in shortening until the mixture resembles coarse crumbs.

2. In a 1-quart glass jar layer in the following order: half of the cereal, the flour mixture, brown sugar, remaining cereal, and the coconut. Tap jar gently on the counter to settle each layer before adding the next one. Seal; attach directions for making Ranger Cookies. Store in a cool, dry place for up to 1 month. Makes 1 jar (enough mix to make about 24 cookies).

PREPARATION DIRECTIONS To make Ranger Cookies: Empty the contents of the jar into a large bowl; stir until mixed. Add 1 beaten egg, 2 tablespoons milk, and 1 teaspoon vanilla; stir until combined. Drop by rounded teaspoons 2 inches apart onto ungreased cookie sheets. Bake in a 375°F oven for 8 to 9 minutes or until edges are golden brown. Cool on cookie sheets for 1 minute. Transfer to wire racks; cool. Makes about 24 cookies.

Viennese Coffee Treat Mix

TO MAKE THE MIX...

2	cups crushed shortbread or chocolate chip cookies
1¼	cups sifted powdered sugar
1	cup chopped nuts
2	tablespoons unsweetened cocoa powder
1½	teaspoons instant coffee crystals or instant espresso powder
¾	teaspoon ground cinnamon

The recipient of this gift will be captivated by the mocha flavor of these sophisticated treats and tickled that no oven is required to make them. For added flavor, lightly toast the nuts before layering them in the jar.

1. In a 1-quart glass jar layer in the following order: crushed cookies, powdered sugar, nuts, cocoa powder, coffee crystals, and cinnamon. Tap jar gently on the counter to settle each layer before adding the next one. If necessary, add additional nuts to fill small gaps in the jar. Seal; attach directions for making Viennese Coffee Treats. Store in a cool, dry place for up to 1 month. Makes 1 jar (enough mix to make about 30 treats).

PREPARATION DIRECTIONS

To make Viennese Coffee Treats:

Empty the contents of the jar into a large bowl; stir until mixed. Add 4 to 5 tablespoons espresso, strong coffee, or water, using just enough to moisten. Form mixture into 1¼-inch balls; roll balls in ½ cup sifted powdered sugar until well coated. Place balls on a sheet of waxed paper; let stand about 1 hour or until dry. Before serving, if desired, roll again in powdered sugar. Store in an airtight container for up to 1 week. Makes about 30 treats.

Fruit and Nut Oatmeal Cookie Mix

Long after the holiday treats are gone, this layered cookie-mix-in-a-jar holds sweet promise for a leisurely day of winter baking.

$3/4$ cup all-purpose flour
$1/2$ teaspoon baking powder
$1/8$ teaspoon baking soda
$1/8$ teaspoon salt
$1/2$ cup butter-flavored or regular shortening
$1/2$ cup packed brown sugar
$1/3$ cup dried tart red cherries
$1/3$ cup golden raisins
1 cup rolled oats
$1/2$ cup chopped pecans or walnuts
$1/4$ cup flaked coconut

1. In a small bowl stir together flour, baking powder, baking soda, and salt. Using a pastry blender, cut in shortening until pieces are pea–size.

2. In a 1-quart glass jar layer in the following order: flour mixture, brown sugar, cherries, raisins, oats, nuts, and coconut. Tap jar gently on the counter to settle each layer before adding the next one. Seal; attach directions for making Fruit and Nut Oatmeal Cookies. Store in a cool, dry place for up to 1 month. Makes 1 jar (enough mix to make about 24 cookies).

PREPARATION DIRECTIONS To make Fruit and Nut Oatmeal Cookies: Empty the contents of the jar into a large bowl; stir until mixed. Add 1 egg and 1 teaspoon vanilla; stir until well mixed. Drop dough by rounded teaspoons 2 inches apart onto ungreased cookie sheets. Bake in a 375°F oven for 8 to 10 minutes or until edges are lightly browned. Transfer cookies to wire racks; cool.

Gingerbread Cutouts Cookie Mix

5   cups all-purpose flour
1   cup sugar
2   teaspoons baking powder
2   teaspoons ground ginger
1   teaspoon baking soda
1   teaspoon ground cinnamon
1   teaspoon ground cloves
    Assorted decorative candies

Dressing up the cookies with decorative candies adds to the fun of holiday baking. Here are some candy suggestions to pack along with the cookie mix: candy-coated milk chocolate pieces, red cinnamon candies, miniature fruit-flavored candies, gumdrops, miniature semisweet chocolate pieces, and/or chocolate-covered raisins.

1. In a large bowl combine flour, sugar, baking powder, ginger, baking soda, cinnamon, and cloves.

2. Divide flour mixture between two 1-quart glass jars. Wrap decorative candies in plastic wrap to make a packet for each jar. Place a candy packet on top of the mix in each jar. Seal; attach directions for making Gingerbread Cutouts to each jar. Store in a cool, dry place for up to 1 month. Makes 2 jars (enough mix in each jar to make 36 to 48 cookies).

PREPARATION DIRECTIONS

1. To make Gingerbread Cutouts: Set aside candy packet from 1 jar. In a large mixing bowl beat $1/2$ cup shortening with an electric mixer on medium to high speed for 30 seconds. Beat in $1/2$ cup molasses, 1 egg, and 1 tablespoon vinegar. Beat in as much of the contents of the jar as you can with the mixer. Using a wooden spoon, stir in the remainder of the contents of the jar. Divide dough in half. Cover and chill about 3 hours or until easy to handle.

2. Grease cookie sheets; set aside. On a lightly floured surface, roll half of the dough at a time until $1/8$ inch thick.

Using a $2^1/2$-inch cookie cutter, cut into desired shapes. Place 1 inch apart on prepared cookie sheets.

3. Bake in a 375°F oven for 5 to 6 minutes or until edges are lightly browned. Cool on cookie sheets for 1 minute. Transfer to wire racks; cool.

4. For icing, in a small bowl combine 1 cup sifted powdered sugar, 1 tablespoon milk, and $1/4$ teaspoon vanilla. Stir in additional milk, 1 teaspoon at a time, until icing is of piping consistency. Decorate cookies with icing and candies from the packet. Makes 36 to 48 cookies.

Trail Mix Bars in a Jar

1¼ cups quick-cooking
rolled oats
⅓ cup coarsely chopped
walnuts or pecans
⅔ cup packed brown sugar
¼ teaspoon ground cinnamon
½ cup semisweet
chocolate pieces
½ cup packaged biscuit mix
⅓ cup dried cherries or raisins
¼ cup shelled sunflower seeds

Looking for a packable gift for an outdoorsy friend? This mix for chewy snack bars is perfect. The baked bars are easy to tote and will cure hunger pangs during almost any outdoor adventure.

1. In a 1-quart glass jar layer in the following order: oats, nuts, brown sugar, cinnamon, chocolate pieces, biscuit mix, cherries, and sunflower seeds. Tap jar gently on the counter to settle each layer before adding the next one. Seal; attach directions for making Trail Mix Bars. Store in a cool dry place for up to 1 month. Makes 1 jar (enough mix to make 16 bars).

PREPARATION DIRECTIONS To make Trail Mix Bars: Grease an 8×8×2-inch baking pan. Empty the contents of the jar into a large bowl; stir until mixed. Add 1 slightly beaten egg, 2 tablespoons milk, 2 tablespoons cooking oil, and 1 teaspoon vanilla; stir until combined. Spread into prepared pan. Bake in a 375°F oven about 25 minutes or until edges are browned. Cool in pan on a wire rack. Cut into bars. Makes 16 bars.

Cherry and White Chocolate Cookie Mix

TO MAKE THE MIX...

1 cup all-purpose flour
$^1/_2$ teaspoon baking powder
$^1/_4$ teaspoon salt
$^1/_8$ teaspoon baking soda
$^3/_4$ cup Vanilla Sugar
1 cup quick-cooking
   rolled oats
$^1/_2$ cup dried tart red cherries
$^1/_2$ cup coarsely chopped nuts
$^1/_2$ of a 10-ounce package white
   baking pieces
$^1/_2$ teaspoon dried lemon peel

The Vanilla Sugar recipe, below, makes a fine gift on its own. Present it in a ribbon-wrapped jar and suggest sprinkling it over baked goods, using it to sweeten cold breakfast cereal or hot oatmeal, or stirring it into coffee or tea.

1. In a medium bowl stir together flour, baking powder, salt, and baking soda. In a 1-quart glass jar layer in the following order: flour mixture, Vanilla Sugar, oats, dried cherries, nuts, white baking pieces, and lemon peel. Tap jar gently on the counter to settle each layer before adding the next one. If necessary, add additional cherries, nuts, or white baking pieces to fill small gaps. Seal; attach directions for making Cherry and White Chocolate Cookies. Store in a cool, dry place for up to 1 month. Makes 1 jar (enough mix to make about 36 cookies).

Vanilla Sugar: Fill a 1-quart jar with 4 cups of sugar. Cut a vanilla bean in half lenghwise and insert both halves into sugar. Secure lid and store in a cool, dry place for several weeks before using. Will keep indefinitely.

PREPARATION DIRECTIONS

To make Cherry and White Chocolate Cookies: Grease cookie sheets; set aside. In a large mixing bowl beat $^1/_2$ cup butter with an electric mixer on medium to high speed for 30 seconds. Beat in 1 egg. Stir in the contents of the jar. Drop by rounded teaspoons onto prepared cookie sheets. Bake in a 375°F oven for 10 to 12 minutes or until edges are lightly browned. Transfer to wire racks; cool. Makes about 36 cookies.

Christmas Biscotti Mix

TO MAKE THE MIX...

2 cups all-purpose flour
2 teaspoons baking powder
³/₄ cup dried cranberries or tart red cherries
³/₄ cup chopped shelled pistachios
¹/₂ teaspoon ground cardamom
²/₃ cup Vanilla Sugar (see recipe, page 22)

Biscotti are Italian cookies that are twice-baked to make them super crisp and ideal for dunking in hot coffee or tea. Create a special presentation by tucking a jar of the biscotti mix in a gift basket with packets of flavored coffees and/or teas.

1. In a small bowl stir together flour and baking powder. In a 1-quart glass jar layer in the following order: dried cranberries, pistachios, flour mixture, cardamom, and Vanilla Sugar. Tap jar gently on the counter to settle each layer before adding the next one. If necessary, add additional dried cranberries or pistachios to fill small gaps. Seal; attach directions for making Christmas Biscotti. Store in a cool, dry place for up to 1 month. Makes 1 jar (enough mix to make about 32 biscotti).

PREPARATION DIRECTIONS

1. To make Christmas Biscotti: Lightly grease a cookie sheet; set aside. In a large mixing bowl beat ¹/₃ cup butter with an electric mixer on medium speed for 30 seconds. Beat in 2 eggs. Using a wooden spoon, stir in the contents of the jar just until combined. Divide dough in half. If necessary, cover and chill dough until easy to handle.

2. Shape each portion of the dough into a 9-inch-long loaf. Place loaves 4 inches apart on prepared cookie sheet; flatten slightly until 2 inches wide. Bake in a 375°F oven for 25 to 30 minutes or until a toothpick inserted near the center comes out clean. Cool loaves on the cookie sheet for 1 hour.

3. Using a serrated knife, cut each loaf diagonally into ¹/₂-inch-thick slices. Place slices, cut sides down, on ungreased cookie sheets. Bake in a 325°F oven for 8 minutes. Turn slices over; bake for 8 to 10 minutes more or until dry and crisp. Transfer to wire

Breakfast Oat Muffin Mix

TO MAKE THE MIX...

1 1/2 cups all-purpose flour
2 teaspoons baking powder
1/4 teaspoon baking soda
1/4 teaspoon salt
1 cup rolled oats
1/2 cup packed brown sugar
3 tablespoons finely snipped candied lemon peel
1/2 cup snipped dried tart red cherries, apples, or apricots
1/3 cup chopped almonds or walnuts

For a thoughtful gift, package a jar of the mix with a muffin tin, decorative holiday paper bake cups, and an oven mitt.

1. In a small bowl stir together flour, baking powder, baking soda, and salt. In a 1-quart glass jar layer in the following order: flour mixture, oats, brown sugar, candied lemon peel, dried fruit, and nuts. Tap jar gently on the counter to settle each layer before adding the next one. If necessary, add additional dried fruit or nuts to fill small gaps. Seal; attach directions for making Breakfast Oat Muffins. Store in a cool, dry place for up to 1 month. Makes 1 jar (enough mix to make 12 muffins).

PREPARATION DIRECTIONS

To make Breakfast Oat Muffins:
Grease twelve 2 1/2-inch muffin cups or line with paper bake cups; set aside. In a large bowl stir together 1/4 cup cooking oil or melted butter, 1 cup milk or one 8-ounce carton vanilla yogurt, and 1 egg. Stir in the contents of the jar. Spoon into prepared muffin cups. Bake in a 400°F oven for 20 to 25 minutes or until a toothpick inserted in the centers comes out clean. Cool in muffin cups on a wire rack for 5 minutes. Remove from muffin cups; serve warm. Makes 12 muffins.

Blueberry Tea Scone Mix

TO MAKE THE MIX...

Dried blueberries can be found in the produce section of larger supermarkets or at food specialty stores.

2 cups all-purpose flour
1/3 cup Vanilla Sugar
  (see recipe, page 22)
1/4 cup nonfat dry milk powder
2 teaspoons baking powder
1 teaspoon dried lemon peel
1/4 teaspoon salt
1/3 cup shortening
1 cup dried blueberries

1. In a large bowl stir together the flour, Vanilla Sugar, nonfat dry milk powder, baking powder, lemon peel, and salt. Using a pastry blender, cut in shortening until mixture resembles coarse crumbs.

2. In a 1-quart glass jar layer flour mixture and dried blueberries. Tap jar gently on the counter to settle contents. If necessary, add additional dried blueberries to fill small gaps. Seal; attach directions for making Blueberry Tea Scones. Store in a cool, dry place for up to 1 month. Makes 1 jar (enough mix to make 10 scones).

PREPARATION DIRECTIONS

To make Blueberry Tea Scones: Empty the contents of the jar into a large bowl; stir until mixed. Add 1 beaten egg and 1/4 cup water; stir just until moistened. Turn dough out onto a lightly floured surface; quickly knead by folding and gently pressing for 12 to 15 strokes or until nearly smooth. Pat or lightly roll dough into an 8-inch circle. Cut into 10 wedges, dipping knife into flour between cuts. Place wedges 1 inch apart on an ungreased baking sheet. If desired, brush tops with milk and sprinkle with coarse sugar. Bake in a 400°F oven for 12 to 15 minutes or until golden brown. Transfer to a wire rack; cool slightly. Serve warm. Makes 10 scones.

Dried Cherry Scone Mix

2   cups all-purpose flour
3   tablespoons sugar
1   tablespoon baking powder
¹/₄ teaspoon salt
6   tablespoons shortening
¹/₄ cup chopped pecans, toasted
¹/₂ cup dried tart red cherries

Treat someone to an easy-does-it breakfast by giving them a decorative basket filled with the fixin's for these delightful scones: the scone mix, a 2-ounce bottle of brandy or an individual-size can of apricot nectar, and a container of Maple-Nut Butter.

1. In a medium bowl stir together flour, sugar, baking powder, and salt. Using a pastry blender, cut in shortening until mixture resembles coarse crumbs. Add pecans; toss. Spoon into a 1-quart glass jar. Wrap dried cherries in plastic wrap; place packet on top of mix in jar. Seal; attach directions for making Dried Cherry Scones. Store in a cool, dry place for up to 1 month. Makes 1 jar (enough mix to make 8 scones).

Maple-Nut Butter: In a small bowl stir together ¹/₂ cup chopped toasted pecans, ¹/₂ cup softened butter, and 1 teaspoon pure maple syrup or maple-flavored syrup. Chill until serving time (up to 3 days). Soften to room temperature before serving. Makes about 1 cup.

PREPARATION DIRECTIONS

1. To make Dried Cherry Scones: In a small bowl combine dried cherries and 2 tablespoons brandy or apricot nectar. Let stand for 15 minutes. Empty the contents of the jar into a medium bowl; make a well in the center of the flour mixture. In another small bowl stir together 1 beaten egg and ¹/₃ cup half-and-half. Add egg mixture and dried cherry mixture all at once to flour mixture. Using a fork, stir just until moistened.

2. Turn out dough onto a lightly floured surface; quickly knead by folding and gently pressing for 12 to 15 strokes or until nearly smooth. Pat or lightly roll dough into a 7-inch circle. Cut into 8 wedges, dipping knife into flour between cuts. Place wedges 1 inch apart on an ungreased baking sheet. Brush tops with 1 tablespoon half-and-half. Sprinkle with coarse sugar. Bake in a 400°F oven for 12 to 15 minutes or until browned. Transfer to a wire rack; cool slightly. Serve warm. If desired, serve with Maple-Nut Butter. Makes 8 scones.

Gingerbread Scone Mix

TO MAKE THE MIX...

3³/₄ cups all-purpose flour
 ¹/₂ cup packed brown sugar
  2   tablespoons baking powder
  2   teaspoons ground ginger
  1   teaspoon ground cinnamon
 ¹/₂ teaspoon salt
 ¹/₄ teaspoon baking soda
 ¹/₄ teaspoon ground cloves
 ¹/₄ teaspoon ground nutmeg
 ³/₄ cup shortening

Gift-wrap a jar of this spicy scone mix with a jar of your favorite honey. The honey is delightful drizzled over warm-from-the-oven scones.

1. In a large bowl combine flour, brown sugar, baking powder, ginger, cinnamon, salt, baking soda, cloves, and nutmeg. Using a pastry blender, cut in shortening until mixture resembles coarse crumbs. Divide flour mixture evenly among three 1-pint glass jars. Seal; attach directions for making Gingerbread Scones to each jar. Store in a cool, dry place for up to 1 month. Makes 3 jars (enough mix in each jar for 6 scones).

PREPARATION DIRECTIONS

1. To make Gingerbread Scones: Empty the contents of 1 jar into a medium bowl; make a well in center of flour mixture. In a small bowl stir together 1 beaten egg, 2 tablespoons milk, and 1 tablespoon molasses. Add egg mixture to flour mixture; stir just until moistened.

2. Turn out dough onto a lightly floured surface; quickly knead by folding and gently pressing for 10 to 12 strokes or until nearly smooth. Pat or lightly roll dough into a 6-inch circle. Cut into 6 wedges, dipping knife into flour between cuts. Place wedges 1 inch apart on an ungreased baking sheet. Brush with milk and sprinkle with coarse or granulated sugar. Bake in a 400°F oven for 10 to 12 minutes or until bottoms are browned. Transfer to a wire rack; cool slightly. Serve warm. Makes 6 scones.

Beer Bread Mix

TO MAKE THE MIX...

1 1/2 cups all-purpose flour
2/3 cup yellow cornmeal
2 teaspoons baking powder
1/2 teaspoon salt
1/2 teaspoon baking soda
2 tablespoons packed
   brown sugar
2/3 cup grated Parmesan cheese
1/2 teaspoon crushed red pepper
4 teaspoons dried minced
   onion or imitation bacon bits

Great served warm with chill-chasing chili or at room temperature for summertime ham or turkey sandwiches, the savory bread made from this mix is a favorite any time of year.

1. In a medium bowl stir together flour, cornmeal, baking powder, salt, and baking soda; set aside. In a small bowl stir together brown sugar, Parmesan cheese, red pepper, and dried onion. In a 1-quart glass jar layer in the following order: half of the flour mixture, Parmesan cheese mixture, remaining flour mixture. Tap jar gently on the counter to settle each layer before adding the next one. Seal; attach directions for making Beer Bread. Store in a cool, dry place for up to 1 month. Makes 1 jar (enough for 1 loaf bread).

PREPARATION DIRECTIONS

To make Beer Bread: Grease an 8×4×2-inch loaf pan; set aside. Empty the contents of the jar into a medium bowl. Add one 12-ounce can or bottle of beer; stir just until combined. Pour into prepared loaf pan. Bake in a 375°F oven for 35 to 40 minutes or until a toothpick inserted near center comes out clean. If necessary to prevent overbrowning, cover loaf with foil for the last 10 minutes of baking. Remove from oven. If desired, brush with butter. Cool in loaf pan on a wire rack for 10 minutes; remove from pan. Serve warm; or cool completely on wire rack. Makes 1 loaf bread (16 servings).

Lemon Tea Bread Mix

3¹/₃ cups all-purpose flour
1¹/₂ cups sugar
   4 teaspoons poppy seeds
   1 tablespoon baking powder
   1 teaspoon salt
   1 teaspoon baking soda
 ¹/₂ teaspoon ground nutmeg

Whether you give the baked bread or a jar or two of the mix, this is the ideal gift for anyone who enjoys entertaining. It's a first-rate addition to any breakfast, brunch, or afternoon tea–party menu.

1. In a large bowl combine flour, sugar, poppy seeds, baking powder, salt, baking soda, and nutmeg. Divide flour mixture between two 1-quart glass jars. Seal; attach directions for making Lemon Tea Bread to each jar. Store in a cool, dry place for up to 1 month. Makes 2 jars (enough mix in each jar for two 5³/₄×3×2-inch loaves or one 8×4×2-inch loaf bread).

PREPARATION DIRECTIONS

1. To make Lemon Tea Bread: Grease bottom and ¹/₂ inch up the sides of two 5³/₄×3×2-inch loaf pans or one 8×4×2-inch loaf pan. Empty the contents of 1 jar into a medium bowl; make a well in center of flour mixture. Set aside.

2. Finely shred enough peel from 1 lemon to yield 1¹/₂ teaspoons shredded peel. Squeeze lemon to yield 2 to 3 tablespoons lemon juice.

3. In a small bowl stir together 1 egg, ³/₄ cup milk, ¹/₄ cup cooking oil, 1 teaspoon of the finely shredded lemon peel and 1 tablespoon of the lemon juice. Add egg mixture all at once to flour mixture. Stir just until moistened (batter should be lumpy).

4. Spoon batter into prepared pan(s). Bake in a 350°F oven for 30 to 35 minutes for the 5³/₄×3×2-inch pans, 45 to 50 minutes for the 8×4×2-inch pan, or until a toothpick inserted near center(s) comes out clean. Cool in pan(s) on wire rack(s) for 10 minutes. Remove from pan(s). Cool completely on wire rack(s). Wrap and store overnight before slicing.

5. Just before serving, combine ¹/₂ cup sifted powdered sugar, remaining ¹/₂ teaspoon finely shredded lemon peel, and enough of the remaining lemon juice (2 to 3 teaspoons) to make an icing of drizzling consistency. Drizzle over the loaf or loaves. If desired, garnish with lemon peel strips. Makes 16 servings.

Cafe au Lait Mix

1/2   cup powdered
      nondairy creamer
1/2   cup buttermints,
      slightly crushed
1/4   cup sifted powdered sugar
2   cups nonfat dry milk powder
2/3   cup instant coffee crystals
     Peppermint sticks or striped
     round peppermint candies

Buttermints add a delightful hint of mint to this coffee-flavored sipper. The mix makes two jars—one to give and one to keep so you can treat yourself during the busy holiday season.

1. In a medium bowl stir together nondairy creamer, buttermints, powdered sugar, and nonfat dry milk powder. In each of two 1-pint glass jars layer half of the powdered sugar mixture and half of the coffee crystals. Insert peppermint sticks or candies as necessary to fill jars snugly. Seal; attach directions for making Cafe au Lait to each jar. Store in a cool, dry place for up to 1 month. Makes 2 jars (enough mix in each jar to make about 5 servings).

PREPARATION DIRECTIONS To make Cafe au Lait: Set aside peppermint sticks or candies. Place 1/4 cup of the dry mix in a mug; add 2/3 cup boiling water. Stir until mix dissolves. If desired, serve with a peppermint stick or candy. Makes 5 servings.

Chai Mix

1¼ cups nonfat dry milk powder
¼ cup black tea leaves
12 pods cardamom
4 2-inch pieces stick cinnamon
2 teaspoons dried lemon peel

If you like, divide the mix between 2 half-pint jars to make 2 gifts. Simply word the gift tag directions to state that each jar's contents should be mixed with 4 cups of water to make 4 servings.

1. In a 12-ounce glass jar layer in the following order: nonfat dry milk powder, tea leaves, cardamom pods, stick cinnamon, and dried lemon peel. Seal; attach directions for making Chai. Store in a cool, dry place for up to 1 month. Makes 1 jar (enough mix to make 8 servings).

PREPARATION DIRECTIONS To make Chai: Empty the contents of the jar into a large saucepan; add 8 cups water. Bring to boiling. Remove from heat. Cover; let stand for 5 minutes. Strain through a wire strainer lined with cheesecloth or a paper coffee filter. To serve, add honey to sweeten to taste. Makes 8 servings.

Spiced Hot Chocolate Mix

TO MAKE THE MIX...

Anise seeds add a hint of licorice flavor to this lively mix that's made by blending semisweet chocolate and cocoa powder.

8   ounces semisweet or
      bittersweet chocolate chunks
      or pieces
²/₃ cup sugar
¹/₂ cup unsweetened
      cocoa powder
¹/₂ teaspoon anise seeds,
      toasted and crushed
¹/₂ teaspoon ground cinnamon

1. In a large bowl stir together chocolate chunks, sugar, cocoa powder, anise seeds, and cinnamon. Spoon into a 1-pint glass jar. Seal; attach directions for making Spiced Hot Chocolate. Store in a cool, dry place for up to 1 month. Makes 1 jar (enough mix to make 12 servings hot chocolate).

PREPARATION DIRECTIONS To make Spiced Hot Chocolate: In a medium saucepan combine ²/₃ cup of the cocoa mix and ¹/₄ cup water. Cook and stir over medium heat until chocolate is melted and mixture is smooth. Whisk in 4 cups milk, half-and-half, or light cream; heat through, whisking occasionally. Pour into mugs. Makes 4 servings.

Raspberry-Fudge Sauce

Raspberry and chocolate are a match made in confection heaven. Can you think of a sweeter way to express your gratitude?

$3/4$ cup unsweetened cocoa powder
$2/3$ cup granulated sugar
$2/3$ cup packed brown sugar
1 cup whipping cream
$1/3$ cup butter
3 ounces bittersweet or semisweet chocolate, finely chopped
3 tablespoons raspberry liqueur

1. In a small bowl stir together cocoa powder, granulated sugar, and brown sugar; set aside.

2. In a medium heavy saucepan combine whipping cream and butter; cook and stir over low heat until butter is melted. Cook and stir over medium heat about 3 minutes or until bubbly around edge. Stir in sugar mixture. Cook and stir for 1 to 2 minutes more or until sugar is dissolved and mixture is smooth and thickened. Remove from heat.

3. Add chopped chocolate and raspberry liqueur to cooked mixture; stir until chocolate is melted. Divide sauce among 3 half-pint glass jars. Seal; attach directions for reheating Raspberry-Fudge Sauce to each jar. Store in the refrigerator for up to 1 week. Makes 3 jars (about 1 cup sauce in each jar).

SERVING DIRECTIONS... To reheat Raspberry-Fudge Sauce: Remove lid from 1 glass jar; microwave sauce in jar on 100% (high) power for 45 to 60 seconds or until heated through, stirring once. (Or empty the contents of 1 glass jar into a small saucepan; warm over low heat.) Serve warmed sauce over ice cream, pound cake, angel food cake, or other desserts.

Caramel-Rum Sauce

TO MAKE THE MIX...

2 cups packed brown sugar
1/4 cup cornstarch
1 1/3 cups half-and-half or
  light cream
1 cup water
1/2 cup light-colored corn syrup
1/4 cup butter
1/4 cup rum
2 teaspoons vanilla

Pair a jar of this sauce with a jar of the Heavenly Hot Fudge Sauce on page 40 for a double treat.

1. In a large heavy saucepan stir together brown sugar and cornstarch. Stir in half-and-half, water, and corn syrup. Cook and stir over medium heat until thickened and bubbly (mixture may look curdled). Cook and stir for 2 minutes more. Remove from heat. Stir in butter, rum, and vanilla. Let stand at room temperature about 45 minutes or until cooled.

2. Divide sauce among 4 half-pint glass jars. Seal; attach serving directions for reheating Caramel-Rum Sauce to each jar. Store in the refrigerator for up to 1 week. Makes 4 jars (about 1 cup sauce in each jar).

SERVING DIRECTIONS... To reheat Caramel-Rum Sauce: Empty the contents of 1 glass jar into a small saucepan. Heat over low heat just until warm. Serve warmed sauce over ice cream, fruit, pound cake, angel food cake, or other desserts. Makes 8 servings.

Heavenly Hot Fudge Sauce

8 ounces semisweet chocolate pieces (1$\frac{1}{3}$ cups)
$\frac{1}{2}$ cup butter
1$\frac{1}{3}$ cups sugar
1$\frac{1}{3}$ cups whipping cream

Chocoholics will rave about this velvety, fudgy sauce. Be sure to keep the heat low while melting the chocolate to prevent it from scorching.

1. In a medium heavy saucepan combine chocolate pieces and butter; cook and stir over low heat until melted. Stir in sugar. Gradually stir in whipping cream. Bring to boiling; reduce heat to low. Boil gently for 8 minutes, stirring frequently. Remove from heat. Let stand at room temperature about 45 minutes or until cooled.

2. Divide sauce among 4 half-pint glass jars. Seal; attach serving directions for reheating Heavenly Hot Fudge Sauce to each jar. Store in the refrigerator for up to 1 week. Makes 4 jars (about 1 cup sauce in each jar).

SERVING DIRECTIONS... To reheat Heavenly Hot Fudge Sauce: Empty the contents of 1 glass jar into a small saucepan. Heat over medium-low heat just until warm. Serve warmed sauce over ice cream, fruit, pound cake, angel food cake, or other desserts. Makes 8 servings.

Luscious Lemon Curd

This old-fashioned lemon curd has an incredible tart and tangy flavor that's sure to delight lemon lovers.

1   cup sugar
1¹/₂   teaspoons cornstarch
¹/₃   cup lemon juice
¹/₄   cup butter, cut up
3   eggs, beaten
4   teaspoons finely shredded
      lemon peel

1. In a medium stainless–steel saucepan stir together sugar and cornstarch. Stir in lemon juice. Add butter. Cook and stir over medium heat until thickened and bubbly. Cook and stir for 2 minutes more.

2. Stir about half of the lemon mixture into the beaten eggs. Return all to the saucepan. Reduce heat; cook and stir for 1 to 2 minutes more or until mixture begins to thicken. Strain to remove any egg particles. Gently stir lemon peel into egg mixture. Divide mixture among four 4-ounce glass jars. Let stand at room temperature for 45 minutes. Seal; attach directions for reheating Luscious Lemon Curd to each jar. Store in the refrigerator for up to 1 month. Makes 4 jars (about ¹/₂ cup curd in each jar).

SERVING DIRECTIONS...

To heat Luscious Lemon Curd:
Empty the contents of 1 glass jar into a small saucepan. Heat over medium-low heat until warm. Serve warmed curd over fresh fruit, pound cake, or angel food cake. Makes 8 servings.

Blueberry Syrup

2 cups fresh or frozen
   blueberries
1/2 cup water
1/3 cup sugar
2 teaspoons lime or
   lemon juice

This not-too-sweet syrup is loaded with whole berries. For two times the pleasure, present it with a box of purchased pancake or waffle mix.

1. In a medium saucepan combine 1 cup of the blueberries, water, sugar, and lime juice. Cook and stir over medium heat for 2 to 3 minutes or until sugar is dissolved. Bring to boiling; reduce heat. Simmer, uncovered, for 15 to 20 minutes or until slightly thickened, stirring occasionally.

2. Stir in the remaining 1 cup blueberries. Cook, stirring occasionally, for 2 to 3 minutes more or until blueberries become soft. Spoon blueberry mixture into 1 half-pint glass jar. Seal; attach directions for reheating Blueberry Syrup to each jar. Store in the refrigerator for up to 1 week. Makes 1 jar (about 1 cup syrup).

SERVING DIRECTIONS...

To reheat
Blueberry Syrup:
Empty the contents of the jar into a small saucepan. Heat over low heat just until warm. Spoon over waffles, pancakes, pound cake, or ice cream. Makes 6 to 8 servings.

Red Pepper Spread

TO MAKE THE MIX...

4   7-ounce jars roasted red
    sweet peppers, drained
1/2 cup tomato paste
4   teaspoons sugar
1   teaspoon dried thyme,
    crushed
1   teaspoon salt
1/2 teaspoon garlic powder
1/8 teaspoon cayenne pepper

This spread features sweet red peppers that have been roasted for a mellow flavor. Garlic and cayenne pepper (the spicy kind!) add just a little kick.

1. In a blender container or food processor bowl combine sweet peppers, tomato paste, sugar, thyme, salt, garlic powder, and cayenne pepper. Cover and blend or process until nearly smooth. Divide pepper mixture among 4 half-pint glass jars. Seal; attach serving suggestions for Red Pepper Spread to each jar. Store in the refrigerator for up to 1 week. Makes 4 jars (about 3/4 cup spread in each jar).

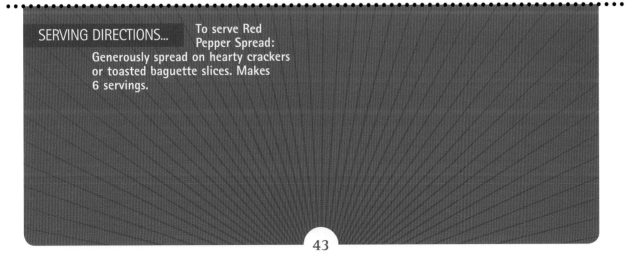

SERVING DIRECTIONS...

To serve Red Pepper Spread:
Generously spread on hearty crackers or toasted baguette slices. Makes 6 servings.

Spinach, Sorrel, and Orange Pesto

It's amazing how versatile a gift of pesto can be! It can be used as a condiment, swirled into soups, or tossed with pasta for a fresh-and-simple side dish.

¹/₄	cup slivered almonds, toasted
1¹/₂	cups loosely packed fresh spinach leaves
1¹/₂	cups loosely packed fresh sorrel, arugula, or watercress leaves
¹/₃	cup olive oil
¹/₃	cup grated Parmesan or Romano cheese
¹/₂	teaspoon finely shredded orange peel
3	tablespoons orange juice
¹/₄	teaspoon cayenne pepper
¹/₈	teaspoon salt

1. Place almonds in a food processor bowl or blender container; cover and process or blend until finely chopped. Add spinach, and sorrel; cover. With the machine running, gradually add oil in a thin, steady stream, processing until the mixture is combined and slightly chunky. Add Parmesan cheese, orange peel, orange juice, cayenne pepper, and salt. Process or blend just until combined.

2. Divide pesto among three 4-ounce glass jars. Seal; attach serving suggestions for Spinach, Sorrel, and Orange Pesto to each jar. Store in the refrigerator for up to 1 week or in the freezer for up to 3 months. Makes 3 jars (about ¹/₄ cup pesto in each jar).

SERVING DIRECTIONS... To serve Spinach, Sorrel, and Orange Pesto: Use as a condiment for sandwiches or grilled meats, swirl into fresh tomato or creamy soups, spread on crostini and top with sliced mozzarella cheese, or tossed with hot pasta. Makes 6 side-dish servings.

Tricolor Tapenade

1/2 cup pitted ripe olives
1/2 cup pimento-stuffed
green olives
1/2 cup purchased roasted red
sweet peppers
2 teaspoons olive oil
2 teaspoons snipped fresh
oregano
1/2 teaspoon black pepper

Tapenade, an olive spread that hails from the South of France, tastes magnificent served over toasted baguette slices. Include a loaf of French bread as part of your gift.

1. In a food processor bowl combine ripe olives, green olives, sweet red peppers, olive oil, oregano, and black pepper. Cover and process with several on-off turns until coarsely chopped. (Or coarsely chop olives and sweet peppers by hand. Stir in oil, oregano, and black pepper.) Divide mixture between two 4-ounce glass jars. Seal; attach serving suggestions for Tricolor Tapenade to each jar. Store in the refrigerator for up to 2 weeks. Makes 2 jars (about 1/2 cup tapenade in each jar).

SERVING DIRECTIONS... To serve Tricolor Tapenade: Use as a spread on freshly baked crostini. For crostini: Cut an 8-ounce loaf baguette-style French bread into 1/2-inch slices. Lightly brush both sides of each bread slice with olive oil; sprinkle with olive oil; sprinkle with salt and pepper. Place on an ungreased baking sheet. Bake in a 425°F oven for 5 to 7 minutes or until crisp and lightly browned, turning once. Top with tapenade. Makes 24 to 30 crostini.

Gazpacho Salsa

3 cups finely chopped tomato
1 cup finely chopped cucumber
1/2 cup finely chopped red onion
1/2 cup finely chopped yellow sweet pepper
1/4 cup snipped fresh cilantro
1 tablespoon red wine vinegar
2 teaspoons olive oil
1/2 teaspoon salt
1/4 teaspoon sugar
1 to 2 small fresh serrano peppers, seeded and finely chopped*
2 cloves garlic, minced

When you use fresh ingredients from your garden or a local farmer's market, this dip really pops with the flavors and colors of summer.

1. In a large bowl combine tomato, cucumber, red onion, sweet pepper, cilantro, red wine vinegar, oil, salt, sugar, serrano peppers, and garlic. Cover and chill for at least 1 hour. Divide tomato mixture among 4 half-pint glass jars. Seal; attach serving suggestions for Gazpacho Salsa to each jar. Store in the refrigerator for up to 2 days. Makes 4 jars of salsa (about 1 cup salsa in each jar).

*Hot peppers contain volatile oils that can burn eyes, lips, and sensitive skin. Wear plastic gloves while working with peppers, and be sure to thoroughly wash your hands afterward.

SERVING DIRECTIONS...

To serve Gazpacho Salsa: Use as a condiment for grilled meats; or serve with tortilla chips, nachos, or toasted pita wedges.

Split Pea Tortellini Soup Mix

⅓ cup dry split peas
3 ounces dried cheese-filled tortellini (⅔ cup)
¼ cup snipped dried tomatoes
½ cup dried chopped carrots
1 tablespoon instant chicken bouillon granules
1 tablespoon dried minced onion
1½ teaspoons dried basil, crushed
1½ teaspoons dried thyme, crushed
½ teaspoon garlic powder
¼ teaspoon black pepper

Soup mugs and a jar of this sensational soup mix make an exceptional gift for even the most hard-to-please person on your gift list.

1. Rinse split peas. Spread split peas in a single layer on paper towels; let stand for 8 to 24 hours or until completely dry.

2. In a 1-pint glass jar layer in the following order: tortellini, tomatoes, split peas, carrots, chicken bouillon granules, minced onion, basil, thyme, garlic powder, and black pepper. Seal; attach directions for making Split Pea Tortellini Soup. Store in a cool, dry place for up to 6 months. Makes 1 jar (enough mix to make 4 main-dish servings).

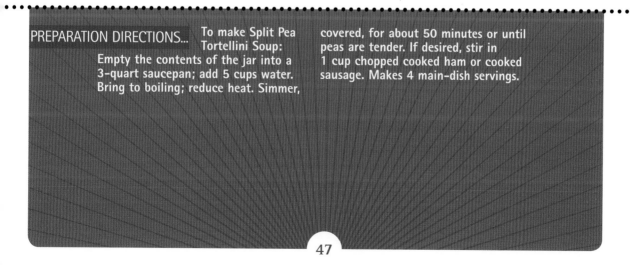

PREPARATION DIRECTIONS... To make Split Pea Tortellini Soup:
Empty the contents of the jar into a 3-quart saucepan; add 5 cups water. Bring to boiling; reduce heat. Simmer, covered, for about 50 minutes or until peas are tender. If desired, stir in 1 cup chopped cooked ham or cooked sausage. Makes 4 main-dish servings.

Lentil Stew Mix

TO MAKE THE MIX...

Keep an extra jar of this herb-seasoned mix on hand to satisfy a spur-of-the-moment craving for homemade stew.

1¼	cups dry green or brown lentils
¼	cup dried minced onion
¼	cup dried green sweet pepper
1	teaspoon salt
1	teaspoon dried thyme, crushed
½	teaspoon fennel seeds, crushed
¼	teaspoon crushed red pepper

1. Rinse lentils. Spread lentils in a single layer on paper towels; let stand for 8 to 24 hours or until completely dry.

2. In a medium bowl stir together lentils, minced onion, sweet pepper, salt, thyme, fennel seeds, and crushed red pepper. Pour mixture into a 1-pint glass jar. Seal; attach directions for making Lentil Stew. Store in a cool, dry place for up to 6 months. Makes 1 jar (enough mix to make 4 main-dish servings).

PREPARATION DIRECTIONS... To make Lentil Stew: In a large saucepan bring 6 cups water to boiling. Stir in the contents of the jar. Return to boiling; reduce heat. Simmer, covered, for 35 to 40 minutes or until lentils are soft. If desired, garnish individual servings with fresh thyme. Makes 4 main-dish servings.

Barley Soup Mix

$^1/_2$ cup dry green or brown lentils

$^1/_2$ cup instant chicken bouillon granules

1 teaspoon dried basil, crushed

$^1/_2$ teaspoon dried oregano, crushed

$^1/_2$ teaspoon dried rosemary, crushed

$^1/_2$ teaspoon black pepper

$^1/_4$ teaspoon garlic powder

1 cup regular pearl barley

$^1/_3$ cup dried minced onion

$^3/_4$ cup chopped dried mushrooms

$^1/_2$ cup snipped dried tomatoes

Greet the first days of autumn with this hearty barley, lentil, and mushroom soup mix. To keep it easy-to-fix, look for roasted chicken in the deli of your local supermarket.

1. Rinse lentils. Spread lentils in a single layer on paper towels; let stand for 8 to 24 hours or until completely dry.

2. In a small bowl stir together chicken bouillon granules, basil, oregano, rosemary, black pepper, and garlic powder. In each of two 1-pint glass jars layer in the following order: half of the lentils, half of the pearl barley, half of the minced onion, half of the mushrooms, half of the bouillon mixture, and half of the tomatoes. Tap jar gently on the counter to settle each layer before adding the next one. Seal; attach directions for making Barley Soup. Store in a cool, dry place for up to 6 months. Makes 2 jars (enough mix in each jar for 6 main-dish servings).

To make Barley–Chicken Soup: Empty the contents of 1 jar into a Dutch oven. Stir in 8$^1/_2$ cups water, 1$^1/_2$ cups chopped cooked chicken (about 8 ounces), and 3 medium carrots, sliced (1$^1/_2$ cups). Bring to boiling; reduce heat. Simmer, covered, for 35 to 40 minutes or until barley is tender. Makes 6 main-dish servings.

Italian Herb and Dried Tomato Risotto Mix

3   tablespoons dried
    minced onion
2   teaspoons dried oregano
1   teaspoon granulated garlic
1   teaspoon dried rosemary,
    crushed
1   teaspoon dried sage leaves or
    dried basil leaves, crushed
$^1/_2$ teaspoon black pepper
$3^1/_2$ cups Arborio rice
$^3/_4$ cup snipped dried tomatoes
8   chicken bouillon cubes

Make this full-flavored risotto mix part of an Italian gift collection by adding a wedge of imported Parmigiano-Reggiano cheese and a bottle of Chianti.

1. In a small bowl combine dried minced onion, oregano, granulated garlic, rosemary, sage, and pepper. In each of 4 half-pint glass jars layer in the following order: one-fourth of the rice, one-fourth of the minced onion mixture, one-fourth of the tomatoes, and 2 chicken bouillon cubes. If necessary, add additional rice or tomatoes to fill small gaps. Seal; attach directions for making Italian Herb and Dried Tomato Risotto to each jar. Store in a cool, dry place for up to 1 month. Makes 4 jars (enough mix in each jar to make 6 side-dish servings).

PREPARATION DIRECTIONS... To make Italian Herb and Dried Tomato Risotto: In a large heavy saucepan bring 3 cups water to boiling. Add the contents of 1 jar. Cook and stir until boiling; reduce heat. Simmer, covered, for 20 minutes (do not lift cover). Remove from heat; let stand, covered, for 5 minutes. Rice should be tender but slightly firm. Stir in $^1/_4$ cup freshly grated Parmigiano-Reggiano cheese.

Wild Rice Pilaf Mix

Although wild rice takes longer to cook than traditional rice, its nutty flavor is well worth the wait.

1   cup wild rice
1   cup regular brown rice
3   tablespoons chopped dried shiitake mushrooms
1   tablespoon instant beef bouillon granules
1   tablespoon dried snipped chives
1   tablespoon dried green sweet pepper or minced dried onion
1½ teaspoons dried basil, crushed
    Black pepper

1. Rinse wild rice. Spread wild rice in a single layer on paper towels; let stand for 8 to 24 hours or until completely dry.

2. In each of 3 half-pint glass jars layer in the following order: ⅓ cup brown rice, 1 tablespoon mushrooms, 1 teaspoon bouillon granules, 1 teaspoon chives, 1 teaspoon sweet pepper, ½ teaspoon basil, ⅛ *teaspoon black pepper*, and ⅓ cup wild rice. Seal; attach directions for making Wild Rice Pilaf to each jar. Store in a cool, dry place for up to 3 months. Makes 3 jars (enough mix in each jar for 4 to 6 side-dish servings).

PREPARATION DIRECTIONS... To make Wild Rice Pilaf: In a medium saucepan bring 1¾ cups water to boiling. Add the contents of 1 jar. Return to boiling; reduce heat. Simmer, covered, for about 40 minutes or until rice is tender and water is absorbed. Makes 4 to 6 side-dish servings.

Jamaican Jerk Rub

2   tablespoons sugar
4½   teaspoons onion powder
4½   teaspoons dried thyme,
     crushed
1   tablespoon ground allspice
1   tablespoon black pepper
1½   to 3 teaspoons ground red
     pepper
1½   teaspoons salt
¾   teaspoon ground nutmeg
¼   teaspoon ground cloves

Ground peppers and sweet spices give this rub a Caribbean kick. Rub it on chicken before grilling for a lively dish that's as easy as a tropical breeze!

1. In a small bowl stir together sugar, onion powder, thyme, allspice, black pepper, red pepper pepper, salt, nutmeg, and cloves. Pour into a 4-ounce glass jar. Seal; attach directions for using Jamaican Jerk Rub. Store in a cool, dry place for up to 6 months. Makes 1 jar (about ½ cup seasoning; enough for 12 pounds of poultry, pork, or fish).

PREPARATION DIRECTIONS... To use Jamaican Jerk Rub: Sprinkle seasoning evenly over poultry, pork or fish; rub in with your fingers. Grill as desired. Cover and store unused seasoning for up to 6 months. Seasons about 8 pounds of poultry, pork, or fish.

Spicy Barbecue Rub

2 tablespoons packed
  brown sugar
1 tablespoon granulated sugar
1 tablespoon ground allspice
1 tablespoon ground ginger
1 teaspoon salt
1 teaspoon ground cumin
1 teaspoon ground red pepper
1 teaspoon black pepper

Spices lose their flavor after about 1 year. To ensure that your gift stays fresh for the 6 months indicated, use spices that have been purchased in the last 6 months.

1. In a small bowl stir together brown sugar, granulated sugar, allspice, ginger, salt, cumin, red pepper, and black pepper. Pour into a 4-ounce glass jar. Seal; attach directions for using Spicy Barbecue Rub. Store in a cool, dry place for up to 6 months. Makes 1 jar (about $1/3$ cup seasoning; enough for about 8 pounds of meat or poultry).

PREPARATION DIRECTIONS... To use Spicy Barbecue Rub:
Sprinkle seasoning evenly over meat or poultry; rub in with your fingers. Grill as desired. Cover and store unused seasoning for up to 6 months. Seasons about 8 pounds of meat or poultry.

2
Chapter

···

Jar Gifts from the Crafts Tables

Clay, fabric, jute, buttons, feathers—there's just no limit on how you can disguise and embellish jars! Clear off your crafts table and get ready to create pretty vases, handy organizers, festive candles, and whimsical banks that are so fun to make the kids will want in on the fun.

Top 10 Crafting Techniques for Jars:

2.

A simple glass canning jar, when adorned with fabric, decoupage, clay, and other colorful items, takes on a whole new look! These handmade treasures make holidays, housewarmings, and birthdays unforgettable.

4a.

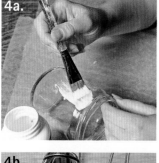

4b.

1. ADD PIZAZZ WITH POLYMER CLAY

Polymer clay, such as Sculpey and Premo, requires oven baking to harden. Colored clay comes in small squares; white is available in large boxes. A bonding agent, such as Liquid Sculpey, is required if clay pieces are applied to the jar before baking. The pieces also can be glued on after baking with a strong adhesive, such as E6000.

2. TRIM WITH AIR-DRY CLAY

Air-dry clay, such as Crayola Model Magic used on the Birdie Bank shown in photo 2 top left is a lightweight clay available in white and colors that dries without baking in the oven. The clay is paintable when dry.

3. PAINT ON COLOR

Glass paints are easy to brush and spray on surfaces. Read the label directions because some glass paints require the painted item to be baked in the oven for the paint to become permanent.

4. ETCH THE SURFACE

Etching gives a frosted look to glass. To etch the entire jar: Brush the exterior of the jar with a thick coat of etching cream as shown in the photo middle left, 4a. Let set according to the manufacturer's directions. Put on rubber gloves. Thoroughly rinse off the etching cream in a sink as shown in photo bottom left, 4b. Let dry. If desired, paint etching cream on jar in simple patterns, such as initials, stripes, or dots.

5. DETAIL WITH DECOUPAGE

Decoupage medium is a glue and topcoat all in one and is available in matte and glossy finishes. Brush it on the jar and cover with small pieces of paper, such as the confetti seen on the Kiddie Canisters shown in photo 5 top of opposite page, cut paper, small photos, or tissue paper pieces. After the pieces are applied to the jar, coat the entire outer surface with more decoupage medium.

5.

6.

6. WRAP WITH TEXTURE

Discover dozens of things to wrap and glue around a jar. The jars shown in photo 5 middle left, are wrapped with jute and banding. Yarn, raffia, braid, ribbon, rope, embroidery floss, and torn fabric strips (when flat and pliable) are other fun options. Choose an adhesive that works for both glass and the decorative trim.

7. COVER IN FABRIC

Instantly disguise jars with fabric. Whether glued to the jar or simply wrapped and tied like the Rose Corsage Vase shown in photo 7 center right, fabrics of nearly any type can dress up a container.

8. SPARKLE WITH GLITTER

When a dazzling effect is desired, coat a jar with decoupage medium or crafts glue and sprinkle with glitter. Other fine crafts supplies work too, such as micro beads and metallic confetti.

9. EMBELLISH WITH LEATHER

Leather and leather lace are available in crafts and hobby stores. These add Western flair to jars when glued or wrapped in place, as seen on the small jar on page 60.

10. SAY IT WITH STICKERS

At a loss for time? Press a border of stickers on jar and the lid! Scrapbooking stores sell decorative stickers with every imaginable theme. For more fun ideas, see the floral foam stickers used on the Birdie Bank on page 78.

7.

Pretty Posy Jar

1-quart canning jar
Disposable plate
Glass paints, such as Liquitex
    Glossies, in yellow, dark red,
    dark green, purple, and white
Dark red paper
1/2-inch flat paintbrush
Round paintbrush
Pencil with round eraser
Scissors

A few simple brushstrokes transform an ordinary jar into a beautiful floral canister.

WHAT TO DO

1. Wash and dry the jar. Avoid touching the areas to be painted.

2. Place a small amount of each paint color on a disposable plate.

3. To make the vertical stripes, double-load the flat paintbrush with yellow and red. Brush once or twice on the plate to slightly blend the colors; the yellow will look more gold. Paint a stripe on the lower half of the jar. Continue the process for each stripe, keeping the dark and light side of the stripes in the same position.

4. Use a round brush to paint petaled flowers, blending dark red with a touch of purple. Paint the flowers above the stripes at different heights.

5. To make the purple flowers, dip the pencil eraser in purple paint and dot on the jar. Dot single or three-petal flowers.

6. Use a round brush to paint purple and green leaves. Let the paint dry.

7. Mix a small amount of dark red in yellow to make gold and paint the centers of the red flowers. Let the paint dry.

8. To make white, purple, and gold dots, dip the paintbrush handle in the desired color of paint and dot on the surface. Let the paint dry.

9. If directed by the paint manufacturer, bake the jar in the oven to make the paint permanent.

10. Remove the insert from the lid of the jar. Place the insert on dark red paper and draw around the shape with a pencil. Cut out the paper circle. Dot the paper with white paint. Let the paint dry. Place the paper and lid insert back into the lid rim.

Natural Solutions

Get organized with storage jars layered with natural fibers, leather lacing, and wood buttons.

Glass jars in various sizes
 with two-part lids
Raw linen or burlap fabric
Tan leather lacing
Wood buttons in desired shapes
Wide jute
1½-inch-wide natural
 cotton banding
Pencil
Scissors
Strong adhesive, such as E6000

WHAT TO DO

1. Remove the insert from the lid of each jar. Place the insert on fabric and draw around the shape with a pencil. Cut out the fabric circle. Glue the fabric onto the top of the insert with adhesive. Let the adhesive dry.

2. Glue the insert into the lid rim using a small amount of adhesive at the edges. Let the adhesive dry. Cut two or three short lenghts from leather lacing; knot in the center and trim the ends. Glue to the center of the jar lid. Let the adhesive dry.

3. For the fabric-wrapped jar, cut a piece of fabric to fit jar, allowing the edges to overlap ½ inch. Fringe fabric ¼-inch on the long edges by gently pulling out threads. Using a thin layer of adhesive to avoid the glue soaking through, glue the fabric around the jar. Choose a button to place on the jar front. Tie some of the pulled fabric threads through the holes; trim. Glue the button to the jar front. Cut a piece of jute to extend from one side of the button to the other; glue in place.

4. For the jute-wrapped jar, glue one end of jute just below the jar threads. Wind the jute tightly around the entire jar, applying glue as you wrap. Cut off the excess jute, securing the end with adhesive. Wrap and glue leather lacing in the crevices of the jute. Let the adhesive dry.

5. For the banding jar, cut two pieces of cotton banding to wrap around the jar. Glue banding strips on the jar, allowing space for three rows of jute between the strips. Glue and wrap jute between the banding strips. Cut approximately eight 1-inch squares from banding. Glue squares on point around the jar, aligning with the top banding strip. Tie on wood buttons with threads from linen fabric. Glue a button in the center of each banding square. Let the adhesive dry.

Mending Jars

4-ounce canning jar
    with 2 piece lid
3-inch square of 1-inch
    crafts foam
$2^1/_4$x$1^1/_4$-inch piece of card stock
5-inch circle of fabric
2-inch square of felt
Felt scraps
18 inches of $^1/_8$-inch-wide
    satin ribbon
Sew-through button
$^1/_2$-inch gold sewing charm
Thick white crafts glue
Thread and needle
Pencil
Pinking shears
Scissors
Items to fill jar, such as buttons,
    needles, thread, thimble,
    safety pins, etc.

Cleverly transform petite canning jars into organizers for mending necessities—such as buttons, needles, and thread.

WHAT TO DO

1. Trace the widest part of the jar band onto foam; cut out. Using thread, gather the outside edge of the fabric circle. Place the circle of foam onto the top of the lid. Add the fabric circle, pulling the gathers tight on the underside, and allowing a $^3/_4$-inch opening. With pinking shears, cut a $1^1/_2$-inch circle of felt .

2. Glue the felt over the gathered fabric on the underside of the lid. Smooth the fabric over the foam, pushing the foam away slightly at the lid edge. Twist on the band.

3. To make the thread and needle holder, use pinking shearscut to cut card stock on the long sides. On one short side, stitch a piece of pinked felt on all sides and slightly larger than the card stock. Allow $^3/_8$ inch of felt to fold over the end of the card stock.

4. Machine-stitch across one end of the felt, securing the card stock.

5. Wrap an assortment of thread on the card stock. Add safety pins at the stitched edge. Insert two needles under the thread into the stitched edge.

6. Fill the jar with sewing notions. Place the ribbon around the neck of the jar. Tie the sew-through button and the sewing charm on the ribbon. Tie the ribbon ends into a bow.

Rose Corsage Vase

WHAT YOU NEED...

1-quart canning jar
1 yard of $7/8$-inch-wide variegated
    deep pink wire-edged ribbon
Wire cutters
Deep pink thread
Two 20-inch-diameter circles of
    light green organza or other
    sheer fabric
24 inches of $1^1/2$-inch-wide green
    wire-edged ribbon
Hot-glue gun and glue sticks

A quart canning jar hides beneath a soft floral covering to create an elegant vase.

WHAT TO DO

1. To make the rose, pull out the wire 2 to 3 inches on one end of the lighter-colored edge of the pink ribbon. Scrunch this end of the ribbon and wrap the wire around the edge to secure as shown in Diagram 1. Pull the wire on the same edge from the opposite end of the ribbon. Pulling gently, evenly space gathers to a length of 12 inches. Scrunch the other end of the ribbon and wrap the wire around it. Cut off the excess wire with wire cutters.

2. Beginning with one end, roll the ribbon end 2 or 3 times. With coordinating thread, sew through the bottom edges to secure. Continue rolling the ribbon, moving the next layer slightly up from the bottom with each roll (see Diagram 2). As you roll the ribbon, sew the edges to the previous layer. For ease in rolling and stitching, hold the rose upside down so the back side faces up. When near the end of the ribbon, fold the edge under (see Diagram 3) and stitch in place. Tie the thread.

3. Evenly gather the organza fabric around the jar and secure at the top of the jar with green ribbon. Knot the green ribbon. Glue the ribbon rose over the knot in the green ribbon.

Diagram 1

Diagram 2

Diagram 3

Harvest Candle Ring

1-quart canning jar with 2piece lid
Gourds, dried ornamental corn,
    pinecones, and strawflowers
    for wreath and jar
Lamp oil
6 inches of fiberglass candlewick
Raffia for bow
Spanish moss
Round twig wreath
    from crafts stores
Hammer and heavy nail
Hot-glue gun and glue sticks

To announce the arrival of autumn, center a colorful canning-jar candle in a twig wreath that overflows with nature's bounty.

WHAT TO DO

1. Arrange gourds, corn, and straw flowers in the jar. Pour in lamp oil to within 1 inch of the jar top. It may be necessary to adjust the contents of the jar slightly as you pour the oil.

2. Use the hammer and nail to punch a hole in the jar lid. Place the lid on the jar; twist on the jar ring. Insert the candle wick. Tie a raffia bow around the neck of the jar.

3. Place a layer of Spanish moss around the wreath and secure it with glue. Arrange and hot glue gourds, corn, pinecones, and straw flowers onto the moss to cover the wreath.

Jam 'n' Jelly Jar Tags

WHAT YOU NEED...

Heavyweight paper or tagboard
Brush pens in desired colors
Metallic gold permanent marker
$1^1/_2$x$2^3/_4$-inch white adhesive labels
Gold elastic cording
$^1/_8$-inch paper punch
Straight or decorative-edge scissors

Made with easy-fit elastic, you can design these colorful tags to go with any occasion.

WHAT TO DO

1. Use straight or decorative-edge sissors to cut the paper into $3^1/_2$×$1^1/_2$-inch strips. If desired, cut the corners off the paper strip.

2. Color the paper strip using a brush pen. Carefully outline the edges of the paper strip using a gold marker. Outline the adhesive label with gold. Center the label on the cut paper strip and press into place.

3. Punch a small hole in each end. Cut a 6-inch length of gold elastic cording. Thread the cording through the hole; knot the ends to secure.

Cute-as-a-Button Luminaries

Canning jars in various sizes
Small colorful nonflammable
        items, such as buttons, candy,
        marbles, and aquarium rocks
Votive candles
Clear glass votive cups

Fill jars with common yet colorful items for a playful presentation of light.

WHAT TO DO

1. Wash and dry each canning jar.

2. Fill the jar one–half to three–fourths full with nonflammable items.

3. Place a candle in a votive cup. Nestle the votive cup in the center of the jar around the nonflammable items.

4. Group several luminaries of varying heights for a dazzling lighted display.

75 Things You Can Put in Jars

It's amazing how a simple glass jar makes a dandy container for everything from game pieces to nuts and bolts. Add a splash of paint, a jazzy ribbon, or let the kids decoupage their favorite pictures on the jar to dress it up.

Address labels	Crayons	Pasta
Air pump needles	Decorative sprinkles	Pencils
Aquarium gravel	Dental floss	Pins and needles
Award pins	Erasers	Playing cards
Bandages	Flowers	Ponytail holders
Barrettes	Game pieces	Popcorn
Bath salts	Gem stones	Postage stamps
Batteries	Golf balls	Potpourri
Beads	Golf markers	Puzzle pieces
Birdseed	Golf tees	Rubber bands
Bobby pins	Gum	Rulers
Bolts	Jelly and jam	Sauces
Bubble blowers	Lipstick	Screws
Business cards	Magnets	Seasoning mixes
Buttons	Make-up brushes	Shells
Candles	Marbles	Silverware
Candle wax	Marshmallows	Small toys
Candy	Matches	Spools of thread
Chalk	Nail polish	Staples
Chocolate chips	Nail punchs	Sugar packets
Combs	Nails	Swimming goggles
Cotton balls	Nuts	Tacks
Cotton swabs	Nail polish	Tea bags
Coupons	Paintbrushes	Toothbrushes
Cough drops	Paper clips	Washers

Turn the Kids Loose and Let the Fun Begin!

Keep little hands busy (and safe!) when crafting with jars. Here are some tips to help along the way.

MAKE IT EASY

The key to any successful crafting project for children is to make it interesting and simple. The following list includes 24 common craft supplies that can be easily applied to a jar:

- air-dry clay
- appliqués
- beaded ribbon
- braid
- buttons
- confetti
- drawings or paintings
- foam stickers
- glass paint
- glitter
- labels
- lightweight wood shapes
- mosaic tiles
- oven-bake clay
- paper quilling strips
- photos
- pipe cleaners
- pom-poms
- ribbon
- rickrack
- stickers
- string
- tissue paper
- yarn

All of these supplies can be purchased at a crafts store.

LET THE CREATIVITY FLOW

Provide children with a canning jar, a bottle of craft glue, and a few of the supplies listed at left and there's no limit to what they can make. For a couple of child-friendly craft ideas, check out the Kiddie Canisters on pages 74–75 and the Birdie Bank on pages 76–77.

PLAY IT SAFE

Whenever children handle glass items, take extra precautions to keep them safe. Here are some tips to share with children when crafting with jars:

- Handle jars carefully. Avoid pressing hard on the jars or forcing on the lids.

- Prevent jars from rolling. When you need to lay a jar on its side, place it on a towel.

- If a jar breaks, avoid touching the broken glass. Ask an adult for help.

Kiddie Canisters

Glass jars with two-piece lids
Paper quilling strips in bright colors
        (available in scrapbooking
        and crafts stores)
Paintbrush
Decoupage medium
Scissors
Strong adhesive, such as E6000

Rainbow-color quilling strips make this bright project easy for the kids!

WHAT TO DO

1. Remove lids from jars; disassemble the lids.

2. For the striped jar, use a paintbrush to cover the top of the lid insert with decoupage medium. Place quilling strips across the top, alternating color strips with black if you wish. Trim the strips around the edge of lid. Brush a coat of decoupage medium on the paper strips and let dry. For the jar, work on small sections at a time. Brush decoupage medium on the jar below the rim. Place quilling strips vertically from the rim to the bottom of the jar, cutting off the excess. Add paper strips until the jar is covered. Brush a coat of decoupage medium on the paper strips and let dry.

3. For the confetti jar, cut several quilling strips into squares. Use a paintbrush to cover the top of the lid insert with decoupage medium. Sprinkle paper squares on the decoupage medium. Brush on more decoupage medium and cover with paper squares until the lid is covered. Brush a coat of decoupage medium on the paper squares and let dry. Apply paper squares to the jar in the same manner. Let dry.

4. To secure the lid inserts to the rims, apply a small amount of strong adhesive at the edges of the insert and press into place. Let dry.

Birdie Bank

1 quart canning jar with 2–piece lid
Air-dry clay, such as Crayola Model
    Magic, in lime green and
    bright pink
Waxed paper
Rolling pin
3-inch foam ball
Ruler
Scissors
Plastic knife
Tracing paper
Pencil
Crafts foam in orange and yellow
2 black map or quilting pins
Assorted feathers
Foam floral stickers
Strong adhesive, such as E6000

Hey kids! Cover a jar with bright air-dry clay and some playful trims to make a super-cool, super-secret bank!

WHAT TO DO

1. Remove the lid insert from the jar lid. Screw the rim piece tightly on the jar.

2. Place a piece of waxed paper on a hard, flat work surface. From green clay, roll a ball slightly larger than a golf ball. Place on waxed paper and flatten with the palm of your hand. Use a rolling pin to continue to flatten the clay until about $1/8$-inch thick.

3. Remove the clay from the waxed paper. Drape the clay over the foam ball, pulling it over the sides to cover the ball. Pinch off the excess clay and smooth the clay with your fingers. Use the smooth part of the clay-covered ball for the top of the bird's head. Roll a quarter-size piece of lime green clay into a ball and press on the top of the bird's head.

4. Using the waxed paper, roll out the remainder of the green clay into a rectangle about 6×14 inches (or large enough to wrap around the jar base, excluding the neck). Press a ruler close to the edge along one long side. Use this line as a guide to trim off the excess clay. Wrap clay around jar

allowing the ends to overlap 1 inch; trim clay as needed. To secure the clay around the jar, overlap the short ends and use the tip of a plastic knife to press the overlapping edges together.

5. Trace the wing, beak, and foot patterns (on opposite page) onto tracing paper. Cut out the shapes.

6. On waxed paper, roll out pink clay to about $1/4$-inch thick. Place the wing pattern on the clay and draw around the shape with a pencil. Turn the pattern over and trace a second wing. Cut out the wing shapes. Use scissors to make small cuts along the bottom edge of each wing.

7. Cut a 2×12-inch strip from pink clay. Placing the seam in the back, wrap the pink clay strip around the jar neck and lid, overlapping the green clay. Allowing the ends to overlap 1 inch, trim off any excess clay. Use the tip of the plastic knife to press the bottom edge of the pink clay to the green clay and to secure the seam at back. Using the photo as a guide, press a wing on each side of the clay-covered jar.

8. With each clay color, roll a pencil-thick rope about 12 inches long. Twist the two colors together and press around the rim of the jar, seam on the back. Cut off any excess clay. Use the excess twisted clay to trim the top of the bird's head. Press into place.

9. To make the beak and feet, trace around the beak pattern on yellow crafts foam and the foot pattern on orange foam. Turn over the foot pattern and trace a second time. Cut out the shapes.

10. Use a plastic knife to press a horizontal indentation on the front of the clay-covered foam ball. Fold the yellow foam beak piece in half. Place the knife in the fold of the beak piece and press it into the indentation on the clay-covered ball. Poke the beak piece into the foam ball until it is secure.

11. Poke feathers in the top of the bird's head and around the wings.

12. Place foam stickers at the top of the bird's head and randomly on the body. Insert black pins above beak for eyes.

13. Glue the feet to the bottom of the jar. Let dry.

14. Let the bird body and head dry separately.

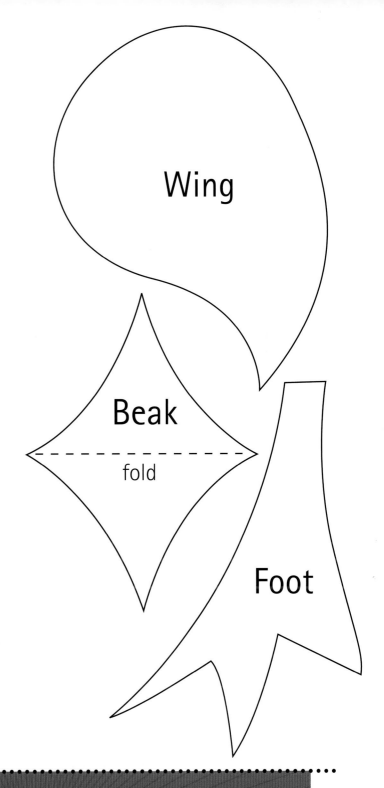

Wing

Beak

fold

Foot

METRIC
INFORMATION

The charts on this page provide a guide for converting measurements from the U.S. customary system, which is used throughout this book, to the metric system.

Product Differences

Most of the ingredients called for in the recipes in this book are available in most countries. However, some are known by different names. Here are some common American ingredients and their possible counterparts:

■ Sugar (white) is granulated, fine granulated, or castor sugar.

■ Powdered sugar is icing sugar.

■ All-purpose flour is enriched, bleached or unbleached white household flour. When self-rising flour is used in place of all-purpose flour in a recipe that calls for leavening, omit the leavening agent (baking soda or baking powder) and salt.

■ Light-color corn syrup is golden syrup.

■ Cornstarch is cornflour.

■ Baking soda is bicarbonate of soda.

■ Vanilla or vanilla extract is vanilla essence.

■ Green, red, or yellow sweet peppers are capsicums or bell peppers.

■ Golden raisins are sultanas.

Volume and Weight

The United States traditionally uses cup measures for liquid and solid ingredients. The chart below shows the approximate imperial and metric equivalents. If you are accustomed to weighing solid ingredients, the following approximate equivalents will be helpful.

■ 1 cup butter, castor sugar, or rice = 8 ounces = ½ pound = 250 grams

■ 1 cup flour = 4 ounces = ¼ pound = 125 grams

■ 1 cup icing sugar = 5 ounces = 150 grams

Canadian and U.S. volume for a cup measure is 8 fluid ounces (237 ml), but the standard metric equivalent is 250 ml.

1 British imperial cup is 10 fluid ounces.

In Australia, 1 tablespoon equals 20 ml, and there are 4 teaspoons in the Australian tablespoon.

Spoon measures are used for smaller amounts of ingredients. Although the size of the tablespoon varies slightly in different countries, for practical purposes and for recipes in this book, a straight substitution is all that's necessary. Measurements made using cups or spoons always should be level unless stated otherwise.

Common Weight Range Replacements

Imperial / U.S.	Metric
½ ounce	15 g
1 ounce	25 g or 30 g
4 ounces (¼ pound)	115 g or 125 g
8 ounces (½ pound)	225 g or 250 g
16 ounces (1 pound)	450 g or 500 g
1¼ pounds	625 g
1½ pounds	750 g
2 pounds or 2¼ pounds	1,000 g or 1 Kg

Oven Temperature Equivalents

Fahrenheit Setting	Celsius Setting*	Gas Setting
300°F	150°C	Gas Mark 2 (very low)
325°F	160°C	Gas Mark 3 (low)
350°F	180°C	Gas Mark 4 (moderate)
375°F	190°C	Gas Mark 5 (moderate)
400°F	200°C	Gas Mark 6 (hot)
425°F	220°C	Gas Mark 7 (hot)
450°F	230°C	Gas Mark 8 (very hot)
475°F	240°C	Gas Mark 9 (very hot)
500°F	260°C	Gas Mark 10 (extremely hot)
Broil	Broil	Grill

*Electric and gas ovens may be calibrated using celsius. However, for an electric oven, increase celsius setting 10 to 20 degrees when cooking above 160°C. For convection or forced air ovens (gas or electric) lower the temperature setting 25°F/10°C when cooking at all heat levels.

Baking Pan Sizes

Imperial / U.S.	Metric
9×1½-inch round cake pan	22- or 23×4-cm (1.5 L)
9×1½-inch pie plate	22- or 23×4-cm (1 L)
8×8×2-inch square cake pan	20×5-cm (2 L)
9×9×2-inch square cake pan	22- or 23×4.5-cm (2.5 L)
11×7×1½-inch baking pan	28×17×4-cm (2 L)
2-quart rectangular baking pan	30×19×4.5-cm (3 L)
13×9×2-inch baking pan	34×22×4.5-cm (3.5 L)
15×10×1-inch jelly roll pan	40×25×2-cm
9×5×3-inch loaf pan	23×13×8-cm (2 L)
2-quart casserole	2 L

U.S. / Standard Metric Equivalents

⅛ teaspoon = 0.5 ml	
¼ teaspoon = 1 ml	
½ teaspoon = 2 ml	
1 teaspoon = 5 ml	
1 tablespoon = 15 ml	
2 tablespoons = 25 ml	
¼ cup = 2 fluid ounces = 50 ml	
⅓ cup = 3 fluid ounces = 75 ml	
½ cup = 4 fluid ounces = 125 ml	
⅔ cup = 5 fluid ounces = 150 ml	
¾ cup = 6 fluid ounces = 175 ml	
1 cup = 8 fluid ounces = 250 ml	
2 cups = 1 pint = 500 ml	
1 quart = 1 litre	